TABLE OF CONTENT

INTRODUCTION   2

THE POWER OF MONEY   3

THE SCIENCE OF LUCK   7

THE SCIENCE OF BEING "LUCKY"   9

MANIFEST MONEY FAST   11

WAYS TO BE LUCKY   14

STRATEGIES TO ATTRACT MONEY INSTANTLY   16

USING THE LAW OF ATTRACTION FOR MONEY EFFECTIVELY   23

THERE IS A SCIENCE FOR SUCCESS   25

INCONCLUSION   26

The author and publisher of this Ebook and the accompanying materials have used their best efforts in preparing this Ebook. The author and publisher make no representation or warranties with respect to the accuracy, applicability, fitness, or completeness of the contents of this Ebook. The information contained in this Ebook is strictly for educational purposes. Therefore, if you wish to apply ideas contained in this Ebook, you are taking full responsibility for your actions.

Thank you for checking out my E-book.

Copyright @ 2017

JCS Finance

Please check out my other Finance E-books at:

http://amzn.to/2tXumYf

INTRODUCTION

Money is a force. It is a concentrated symbol of energy and power in life. Like all forces in the universe, money obeys certain universal laws or principles. By understanding those laws and acting appropriately, we gain a great power over money, enabling wealth and prosperity to come our way.

Most of us are aware of the importance of hard work, determination, and drive to attract money. However, there are also other, more hidden and subtle ways to attract money, wealth, and prosperity. When followed, these methods have a tendency to instantly attract money from seemingly out of nowhere, defying our normal notions of cause and effect, and what is logical and possible. Such sudden and abundant results are indications of the wondrous phenomenon of "life response" at work.

Money is a source of power and status. People who make a lot of money also have a lot of money to spend. We always considered this to be a powerful people. A lot of money allows people to control other people as well.

Do you know that not all powerful people are rich; some have been very poor. Like our dear Mother Theresa, the nun who worked tirelessly to care for the world's poorest and most desperate people. She did all these as it came from her courage and conviction and most importantly from the love of her heart.

Being lucky could mean a lot of things to a lot of people. What I am talking about here is being lucky in life, not lucky in the lottery or any other form of gambling, as this is down to chance alone. Being lucky in life is when you have the life you want and it seemingly happens by accident, by pure luck.

Finding money on the street may seem like a lucky break, but it might be more accurate to thank yourself. Researchers across various disciplines have attempted to decode whether there's an actual measurable aspect to what we understand as luck. Many of these studies have found that what a person might perceive as "luck" has more to do with psychology than probability; "luck" is actually just her own positive attitude that keeps her open to new opportunities or perceiving patterns in random acts of chance.

THE POWER OF MONEY

Money can entice one to all kinds of sin; in fact, there is almost no sin imaginable to which it does not entice. However, this is merely the consequence of the core corruption money brings as soon as it becomes for someone what his God alone can and may be for him. That struggle also goes on for a long time in the heart. Our human heart needs a point of support on which to depend, rest, lean, and rely and from which it derives the peace, rest, and calm of life. At first, things fluctuate. At one time the heart finds this support in God, at another time in money or capital. As long as these threats can be countered with money, God takes second place. But if the threatening affliction or danger takes on a character against which gold can no longer fight, then in most people our God's name once again rises to the surface as the heart again seeks comfort in the God it had forgotten.

For many, their adherence to money gradually becomes so dominant that it begins to rule their entire soul and all their senses. The more money people have at their disposal, the more assured and certain they feel in their capacity for managing such a monetary treasure. They begin to look down almost in pity on those poor souls who have hardly any money and who seek consolation in prayer and thanksgiving and in their dependence on a purely imaginary God. They do not begrudge them this, since these poor souls after all need something in order to keep going in their poverty-stricken state. The rich, however, feel themselves to be beyond that. Those poor souls chase after a dream, while these folk hold on to reality.

The contrast thus becomes sharper and sharper. Religion is for the poor and destitute who gaze at mere semblances, but money and gold constitute the real power for those with possessions. It is their rock, their support, and their strength. In this way, money first comes to stand beside religion; then there follows a period when money drives religion out of the heart; and in the end, a mystical veneration for money itself arises in the heart. At first one serves both God and mammon. Then the soul becomes entirely monetized until all religion appears to be erased. In the end, not only the worship of God falls away forever, but under a different form something of that old worship reappears and develops into a sort of religious veneration of money and mammon. This is exactly how Christ said things would go. First, you try to serve both God and mammon. This cannot be done, however, and is impossible in the long run. You cannot serve God and mammon. For that reason, if you do not want to break with mammon, the religion of your God can only die off in your monetized heart, so that in the end nothing remains but the money-god, mammon.

The sad process that affects individuals addicted to money becomes reality for entire social circles and even countries. Especially those countries that are devoted to the business of wholesale trade and banking experience over time the incredible power that money has. In that way, they ultimately become so impressed by that enormous world power that only in periods of high spiritual elevation in the circles of this powerful commercial world does one still see a religious tone reign.

Over the course of the last century, this ugly phenomenon has spread out in ever widening circles and has gradually assumed a worldwide character. World life in its entirety now stands under the sign of money-power. In the international community there is hardly any sensitivity for higher interests anymore. Almost all governments openly show that their only goal is to increase their population's riches and welfare. This orientation in government policy has pushed material and financial interests to the foreground. All conflicts between states, whether they involve war or not, aim at obtaining the greatest possible financial advantages for their own country. This spirit has penetrated downwards and placed its grasp on all levels of society. The battle, the fierce struggle of the so-called proletariat against capital, had no other cause. From those wide circles the same thirst for money worked its way into families and people. The lust of the current generation is to accumulate wealth, to better one's position, and to have at our disposal the greatest amount of money possible.

It is no longer the man from a family of high standing, the man of character and high intelligence, the man of noble spirit, who presides at the nation's table. The place of honor is now reserved for the merchant, for the one who has much money, for the millionaire. This passion has proved itself to be so infectious that even families of standing have cast their higher calling aside and now strive to match the financial power of the nouveau riche; yes, even kings and princes exert themselves to earn honor and respect among the money magnates by acquiring as much capital as the magnates do— or even more. Without wealth you are nothing. All doors are open to those with immeasurable capital, and so they automatically climb higher and higher on the social ladder. Wealth covers everything; without wealth you are helpless.

How could the worship of him who created heaven and earth ever survive when faced with the enormous growth of money's power in the unregenerate human heart? Worship of the only true God reaches very deep. It does not tolerate you placing your confidence in some creature, in something other than him alone. However, we are faced with a mystery at this point. It pleased God in his unsearchable design to allow the power of money to establish its throne on earth and to wave its scepter over the kingdom of this world. And let us not hide the truth in money, there rules a power that closely approaches God's omnipotence, at least insofar as the satisfaction of the needs and wants of one's outer life is concerned. God himself mysteriously raised that power to life in order to confront us more than ever before with the choice for or against him. After all, you can expect all you desire from the power of money; you can ask and receive it from mammon. This places you before the question that your God asks you in your conscience: Is it your determined choice to reject all these things, to recognize that they are nothing, and to place your only, unwavering, and full trust in me as your God?

5 Steps to Manifest More Money with the Law of Attraction

Law of Attraction Teaches Almost everyone I know wants to know how they can increase their cash flow. Perhaps you have questioned why some people seem to always have money while others struggle just to make ends meet.

I think it is safe to say that most of the world uses and needs money to survive. Although everyone uses and needs money, not everyone has a healthy view about money. Many religions teach that money is the "root of all evil". They hold on to cliché's such as "the rich are getting richer while the poor are getting poorer.".

If you want more money in your life, then you've got to show money love. This may sound strange to you, but the law of attraction simply stated says "like attracts like".

Attracting money into your life is much like a love relationship. If you want to attract that sexy woman or that handsome guy into your life, then you call them on the phone. You meet together on a dinner date.

Perhaps you write love letters or sweet poems. You find out what the person likes and make a little surprise gift. You keep a picture of that person in your wallet. You are in love. This is basically what the law of attraction is about. It's not just saying or writing affirmations. It's not just using pictures to visualize things. It's putting your whole heart, soul and mind into it.

With money, it has to be the same way. First step to attracting money is;

1. Realize money is like electricity. In of itself, it is not good or evil. Much like electricity, you can use it to do a lot of good or cause a lot of unhappiness. Many people blame money for their mistakes and are afraid to face responsibility for their own life.

2. Everything that you want to manifest requires a specific spirituality accordingly. Spirituality is an intense feeling for something. It is a healthy and balanced love for something. If you are afraid to love money, how can you ever expect it to want to come to you? Remember, this is a healthy and balanced love.

3. Keep pictures or symbols of money to help you focus and remind you of your intention. You can use pictures of money, real money, or symbols such as rocks or marbles. Use whatever works best for you.

4. **Take action.** Don't just take an action for action's sake, but meditate and think it through. Trust your sub consciousness to lead you to do the right action, but nonetheless don't expect for things to just fall out of the sky into your lap.

5. **Imagine.** Use your imagination of what you would feel like if you were wealthy. Exactly how much money would you like to have? When? Make it crystal clear into your mind and then work with the feeling of already having it now. I recommend this should be done on a daily basis for at least half an hour, but again, do what works best for you. Remember that you want to do this regularly and you want this to be a fun thing, not a chore.

THE SCIENCE OF LUCK

Finding money on the street may seem like a lucky break, but it might be more accurate to thank yourself. Researchers across various disciplines have attempted to decode whether there's an actual measurable aspect to what we understand as luck. Many of these studies have found that what a person might perceive as "luck" has more to do with psychology than probability; "luck" is actually just her own positive attitude that keeps her open to new opportunities or perceiving patterns in random acts of chance. Here are some of the latest findings.

Games of Chance

You just flipped four heads in a row, so the next one has to be tails, right? Wrong—the odds of flipping heads or tails is still

50/50, exactly the same as it has been every other time. This is called the "gambler's fallacy," and, according to a study published earlier this month in PNAS, our brains may be seeking out these sorts of patterns. "A major function of the human brain is to deal with the uncertainty in the real world in order to find regularities," says Yanlong Sun, a professor of microbial pathogenesis and immunology at Texas A&M College of Medicine and one of the study authors. Our neurons detect these patterns naturally and pay special attention to their timing, Sun says. Neurons prefer alternating pattern it's the brain's way of "regressing to the mean," to correct for patterns that seem statistically unlikely. "Our study shows that our brains are probably smarter than we previously have thought, in that they are able to automatically pick up some very subtle yet important statistical structures in the environment," he says. But this new understanding doesn't change how Sun feels about luck overall "As both a scientist and a person, I do believe in luck, that it is something I cannot manipulate or operate on. "As both a scientist and a person, I do believe in luck."

Lucky Streaks

When you're placing bets on a game like craps or roulette that is based on chance, it turns out that your betting shifts your odds. A person who wins two bets in a row has a 57 percent chance of winning the next one, but a person who has lost two bets in a row has only a 40 percent chance of winning the next. Why? According to a study published last year, people again fear that their bets will regress to the mean that if they won, they are more likely to lose the next time, so they compensate for it by making safer bets each successive time.

When people who have been winning take safer bets, it means they'll probably keep winning; when people have been losing, they take riskier bets to try to win, which means they actually lose more. The actual event the gambler bets on doesn't become any more or less probable, but past outcomes affect how the bettor allocates funds the next time around.

Superstitions

Crossing your fingers, knocking on wood most of us don't know where superstitions like these came from, even if a lot of us practice them fairly often. But several studies show that superstitions might work, though not in the way that we think they do.

In one, from 2010, golfers who were told that they were using a "lucky ball" performed significantly better than those who were told that theirs was "the same ball everyone else had used so far." The test subjects also performed better when they were allowed to hold on to their "lucky charms" from home while solving an anagram problem. The researchers hypothesized that the people with their luck charms by their side persisted at problems longer because they felt more effective, like they had the assistance of some other power. It's the same logic that Alcoholics Anonymous has used to help people get sober and stay that way people feel empowered when they think that someone else is helping them, so they actually do better at the tasks at hand.

Lucky People

Luck doesn't just "happen," even for people who consider themselves lucky. Richard Wiseman, a professor of psychology at the University of Hertfordshire in England, has done a number of studies to figure out what distinguishes a lucky person from an unlucky one. In one study, he asked people who identified as luck and as unlucky to read a newspaper. On one half page of a newspaper, he wrote in large letters: "Tell the experimenter you have seen this and win £250." The people who said they were lucky were more likely to see the ad, Wiseman wrote, and the "unlucky" people seemed to demonstrate more anxiety, which detracted from their powers of observation. Now, Wiseman has "four principles" of luck on his web site, and they all have to do with being open to new experiences and observing opportunities as they present themselves.

THE SCIENCE OF BEING "LUCKY"

Everyone knows that one person who has seemingly gotten more than their fair share of lucky breaks in life. It could be the coworker who jumped into a higher-up position as soon as it opened, the relative who made a life-changing career switch, or an investment that paid off, and paid off well.

And it's easy to look at that person who's tackling big hurdles and flying over them with ease, while you're diligent and hardworking but taking baby steps up the success ladder, and think "Man, are they lucky."

Well, it's naturally important to remain diligent and approach every job or task with a sense of excellence, but sometimes the difference between the "lucky" guy and the simply "hardworking but reliable guy" comes down to one thing urgency.

Why Urgency?

To be a winner, you need to be excellent, but you also need to be able to identify opportunities and act with a sense of urgency to understand the magnitude of the moment, and sweep in accordingly. After all, waiting for a "ship to come in" will always result in an empty harbor.

Let's take a look at a couple examples.

For the coworker who was immediately granted a higher position as soon as it was available, there's a good chance that as soon as they heard about the opening, they approached their superiors with a presentation on how they were instrumental to the company, and what they could do to expand the company's profit and / or productivity in this new role.

For the relative who made a life-changing career switch, odds are that they prepared in advance to be ready, such as by learning a new skill so when the opportunity presented itself, they could seize it before it dissipated.

Now does this mean that you should ☐uit your day job right now and open up that juice bar you've always dreamed about? Not just yet!

Let's Talk About Urgent Excellence

By urgent excellence, I mean we need to strive to be excellent in everything we do, but we also need to feel a sense of urgency not anxiety which motivates us to act.

Urgent excellence effectively comes in three parts:

You recognize the opportunity: An opportunity is much different than a gauzy wish list it's in front of you, and it's obtainable, and taking the leap doesn't necessarily cause a feeling of panic or anxiety. A bad feeling isn't a good start to any new endeavor.

You respond swiftly and seize the moment: Opportunities are obvious. You'll feel it in your gut, and you'll know if it will propel you forward. Don't hem and haw and look for all the little downfalls, because if you look hard enough, you'll surely find them with any new change. Instead, grab hold, and use your sense of excellence and diligence to go forward.

You'll reap the rewards: Once you secure your opportunity, don't slow down your hard work and diligence is what connected you with the opportunity in the first place, and it's what will transform an opportunity into a success story that your friends will someday deem "lucky."

As in our example above about the prepared relative most successful people who seem "lucky" worked hard to prepare themselves so when #1 happens (recognition of the opportunity), they are in a position to be able to act on it and act with urgency.

MANIFEST MONEY FAST

Manifest money is a process of adopting new empowering beliefs that will allow you to shift your vibration. As your, vibration begins to change, you develop yourself into a suitable container for money, abundance, and prosperity. Think of it this way, and you would never pour water into a paper bag. A paper bag is not a fitting container for liquids. Glass, however, is perfect for holding water. The only ꞏuestion left to ask is if the glass you hold is large enough for the amount of water you want to drink? Individuals with a poverty mindset spend most of their time attracting poverty. Remember when it comes to the Law of Attraction, likes to attract likes. 100% of the time a scarcity mindset is held because of a person's core beliefs and values.

Next, we get to the idea of speed. The gunk that slows down the gears of attracting money fast is limiting belief and fears. Both are negative lower vibrational feelings. Both are damaging to obtaining money quickly. Both can be changed with new and empowering beliefs.

Throughout history those who have attracted large amounts of abundance and money have made massive changes to the way they think, beginning with their beliefs.

These changes of mind are responsible for incredible stories from the life of people like Walt Disney, to Colonel Sander. Winners, in every endeavor in life, invoke extreme change simply by changing their thoughts. This shift ultimately transforms their energy field and what they attract. The following are seven secrets you can begin to employ today to attract money fast into your life. These are tested principals that always work.

Set clear Intentions and goals.

The Universe becomes a far more active partner in helping you create the life you desire when your intentions are specific. You don't just want money fast; you want X amount of dollars fast or even more. Once I walked into a casino with only $1.00 in my pocket, having forgotten my wallet at home. Amazingly, I walked out of the casino with a sizeable sum of money. I set an intention that I wanted to turn that dollar into $20.00. I could have driven home to get my wallet, but I was already there and decided to invoke the power of the Law of

Attraction. By the time the dust settled that day, I had won $2400! Remember, I started with only $1.00

Invoke the power of your subconscious mind.

There are many tools you should be using from creative visualization to affirmations and incantations. You must bury your mind in your desires, and new belief. The more you do this, the better. Make your new statements and beliefs an entire lifestyle. Continue to raise your standards and expect more from yourself daily.

Feel the Money.

Fill your mind with thoughts of already having the money you need in your wallet or bank account. Imagine driving your new car, or living in your new home, or taking your dream vacation. About ten years ago I had the urge to travel to India. I began burning Indian incense, listening to Indian music, eating Indian food. I employed the power of the Law of Attraction. Within two months I was provided an entire trip to India, with a 5-star hotel, tours, everything I had imagined and even more. I met and studied with deeply spiritual people. It was a fantastic journey and a life changing experience. The entire trip was attracted through my ability to feel the money. In this case, I experienced the trip in my mind, and the money was provided to take the journey.

Send Energy to Your Intention for FAST MONEY.

There are many ways to do this. In this point, I will share one method that has proven to be extremely useful.

Step One: Clear some space in an area of your house. Burn some cleansing incense such as Sage, or Frankincense, or even Sandalwood. When it comes to money, I learn in the direction of sandalwood.

Step Two: Light four candles in the four corners of your room. These candles serve as the light and as also symbols that you are pulling metaphysically from all four directions and all four elements, Air, Fire, Water, and Earth.

Step Three: Stand in the center of your space and close your eyes with your hand out, palms facing each other as if holding a ball of light. Visualize the light growing in between your hands. Fill this ball of light with your intention. One way to do this is to recite your affirmation into the ball of light and feel your affirmation growing in power and intensity. Manifest money fast

Step Four: Release the ball of light with your intention upward into the heavens. With your eyes still closed visualize the ball of light exploding in the heavens and causing it to rain gold coins all around you. Feel the money, see the gold, and allow the excitement to fill your body with enthusiasm. Wealth, prosperity, and money are flowing to you from the INFINITE FIELD, THE UNIVERSE.

Recite these two special affirmations in addition to other affirmations you may already be using:

"Money is too easy to make."

"Money comes to me easily and quickly."

Respect the Money you already have.

Look at the money in your wallet or on your computer, open to your back account and check your balance. No matter how little or small be grateful for the balance, and respect it. You can even say to your money; I respect you so much that I desire more of you, and you and I will work in harmony to accomplish the things important to me.

Let it flow and let it go.

Take daily action by doing your spiritual and inner work. Once you have begun taking action, stop thinking about it, stop worrying, and just allow your money to flow. Often the more you think about it, the slower the money flows. You will attract money fast when you let it go and let it flow using the power of the Law of Attraction.

WAYS TO BE LUCKY

I work with someone who seems incredibly unlucky in everything she does. If something unlucky is going to happen it will happen to her. She is a manic person whose mind is constantly racing and she tries to do 100 things at once. When she talks it's at 100 miles per hour, she asks questions about 5 times before taking it in, she is distrustful of people, she sees the bad in everyone and to top it off she's a very nice person. However, she must be the unluckiest person I have ever met.

In contrast I know someone else who seems to be incredibly lucky. He is optimistic, sees the good in people, believes that good things will happen to him and his family and regularly has conversations about the good things he wishes for himself and his family. He knows what he wants and he goes after it with all guns blazing. Yet he is laid back, he is a very kind and generous person and is happy in life.

People who are lucky show certain characteristics and beliefs about themselves and the world so I would like to share with you the eight ways to be luckier.

7 ways to be luckier

Belief: Believing that you will get the things you want in life and deserve the things you want in life will make you more prone to receiving them. Why is this? When you think about something you see a picture in your head, when you have a picture in your head your mind is locked onto receiving it. When you mind is locked onto receiving something it will start, unconsciously, to notice ways of getting what you want.

It will start to notice opportunities that you might have missed had you not had that picture in your head and the belief it could happen.

Taking risks: People who are lucky take more risks. This doesn't mean they gamble their house and take risks on new businesses and forgetting their family. Taking a risk can be calculated, you weigh up your options know what you can afford to lose and go for it. If it doesn't work out you go for it again when you can afford to lose more.

Working hard: A lot of sports stars, singers, dancers, actors etc seem to have become famous overnight and are rich beyond belief. However what most people don't see is that those same people have spent years of hard work and sacrifice to get to where they are today. Take Sylvester Stallone, he auditioned with every casting agency he could and didn't get anywhere until he wrote a script for Rocky, and the rest is history. Working hard is a pre-re uisite to being lucky.

Generosity: Being generous to others seems to be a trait in all lucky people. They give generously of their time and their money. They share their luck and wealth among others. A lot of people share their knowledge which can be more valuable than money or time. I have met so many people through this blog and I believe it's because I share what I know and what I have learned throughout my life and throughout the research I have done over the years.

Instinct: Listening to your instinct can be invaluable when it comes to choosing what you want in life. How many times have you had the instinct to go for something but your brain held you back and told you all the reasons not to do it, then later on you find out it would have worked out well after all. We all have instincts for a reason and some people take more heed when it comes to listening to their instincts, you can hone this ability simply by listening with your body, be aware of your bodily sensations when you are thinking about trying something new. The more you trust your instinct the more it will serve you better.

Positive outlook : Having a positive outlook on life is a must if you are to become a luckier person. If you outlook on life is doom and gloom then I am afraid to say this is how you will see life itself. Your brain thinks 'I am a gloomy little git, so I will look for things to be gloomy about' whereas if you have a positive outlook your brain will say 'I am a cheery little git, I will look for more things to be cheery about'. You control what is input int your brain by your thoughts, change your thoughts and you will change your life.

Coping with bad luck: The way you cope with bad luck can change your life, If something bad happens to me I always look at what could have made that situation worse. Two weeks ago my washing machine, power shower and gas all packed up at the same time. It was going to cost over £700 to get them all fixed. Luckily, my wife had taken out a gas plan 1 week previous and we were covered for the repairs which would have cost us hundreds. We managed fine with a bath, and are still doing so, and we bought a new washing machine which was on special offer at the time, how lucky was that. Being lucky does not happen by luck it happens by having a positive attitude in life, working hard and sharing yourself with others. This has been proven in numerous studies and time and time again it has been shown that changing your thoughts really does change your luck.

STRATEGIES TO ATTRACT MONEY INSTANTLY

Attention

It is a basic law of life that everything whether it is a physical object or a human being responds to greater attention. Money is no exception. The best way to give attention to money is to account for it accurately and in a timely manner. Keeping precise and up-to-date accounts of money is a powerful mechanism for suddenly attracting more of it.

One small business owner balanced eight months of back bank statements in a weekend, and received $5000 from nowhere the next day.

An individual noticed that an idle machine had become run-down, so he decided to clean and fix it. Within a few days, a new work project suddenly sprung up where this very machine was required. The project, using that machine, became a huge new source of income for the business.

Circulation

Like any force, money needs to move freely in order to sustain itself. Holding back on paying, or otherwise hoarding money, prevents the free flow of energy, and thus the free flow of money. For example, we have seen a number of instances where individuals were unwilling to pay the bills they owed until they first received payments of money due to them. Reversing such an attitude can bring a sudden abundant positive response from life.

A programmer, who had little cash on hand, was unwilling to write out checks for current bills due until he received money owed him from his clients. He had been waiting for a number of days for this payment to come in. He then reversed his attitude, and went ahead and wrote out the checks for the money he owed anyway. When he went to pick up his mail ten minutes later, he was surprised to discover the check he had yearned for in his mailbox.

We have also seen instances where individuals were unwilling to spend their current funds for important necessities. Even when they had plenty of cash on hand, they hoarded it, often because of some unfounded fear. When they reversed themselves, life responded in extraordinary ways.

A web site owner was hesitant to upgrade to a better web site because of the added expense, even though he had the required funds. The web host provider had suggested the better site a number of times in the past. When the web site owner finally overcame his reluctance to spend, he discovered to his surprise that the web host provider had suddenly, the day before, begun offering this better, higher-priced site, at a cost virtually the same as his current site!

There was a man who was hesitant to spend money on a deserving friend. When he changed his position and did so, he saw that money came back to him in the exact amount he had spent on his friend!

If you give up such attitudes and let money circulate, energy will flow, and life will reward you with good fortune, including the constant flow of money in your direction. This is the proof of the subtle principle of "inner-outer correspondence"; i.e. life reflects on the outside your psychological condition inside yourself. If you make your feelings or attitudes more positive, such as overcoming an unwillingness to pay a bill or the hoarding of money, life on the outside will respond positively to you in kind.

Long-term Debt Owed

Very often those who suffer from money problems have borrowed in the past and have forgotten to repay, even when they had the opportunity to do so.

One individual owed friend money for over twenty years. An instance after he committed to paying off the old debt, he received news that he had been offered a better place to live, after having lived in the same cramped apartment for over twenty years! In addition, he experienced a sudden surge in his workload, which included higher-paying type work.

We see from this example how very important it is that you pay off old outstanding debts. Not doing so may very well prevent you from ever moving beyond your current situation.

Sums Owed to You

It is also important to collect all money owed to you, including the minutest of sums. If you do so, money will suddenly come to you from all directions.

An individual understood that one should not neglect collecting even the smallest amount owed to one. He then decided to practice it CONSCIOUSLY, and see for himself what would happen. So he collected even the smallest amounts due to him from others (such as 10 cents and 20 cents!). After he successfully collected on these, in the following few days he received Rs.300, 000 ($7,500) for various receipts coming from unexpected sources.

An individual had exhausted his bank account. He was in desperate straits. He remembered that if he collects every penny still due to him, money can come. He then contacted the sole debt he had on his books, which went back nearly six years! He contacted that person to secure the payment. The next morning he received a most unexpected purchase and payment from another source that instantly resolved his quandary.

Taking Care of Neglected Duties

There are circumstances where money will not come your way until you take care of neglected areas of your life. Once you give those areas the attention they deserve, money or other good fortune can instantaneously come your way.

A payment for new services rendered was anticipated by a software company, but got delayed for various technical reasons. The individual in charge remembered that several older clients had still not sent their payment. He had neglected to stay on top of that matter. Now with the current situation of the new potential client, he felt there was a correlation between the receivables he neglected to keep on and the new payment that was having technical problems coming in. Thus, he immediately contacted both of the older clients that owed receivables to find out their latest status. Instantly, thereafter (literally within seconds of hanging up on the phone with the older clients) the money for the new client was properly cleared and came in.

Cleanliness, Orderliness

Perhaps the simplest and most dramatic way to attract money is to raise your level of physical cleanliness at home or at work. Many individuals and businesses have followed this practice, and seen money suddenly rush in from all sides, often from the most unlikely sources!

An instructor had not been contacted for new work for weeks, and was in desperate straits. He decided to apply the principle of higher cleanliness. His apartment was normally clean, but he wanted to take cleanliness a step further. So he decided to clean his refrigerator; something he was ordinarily reluctant to do. At the exact moment he finished putting the foodstuffs back into the refrigerator after the cleaning, he heard a message on his answering machine from his training company offering him abundant new work. The response from life was instantaneous to the completion of the cleaning!

A consultant suggested that before he made any business recommendations to his client that they immediately clean up their showroom and backyard area. Time passed. The next time the consultant visited the company, he learned that there had been an unexpected sudden surge in new orders. This came just after the company implemented the consultant's advice about cleanliness.

We recommend that anyone looking to attract more money take up this strategy immediately. There is no faster way to attract positive good fortune -- including fresh new sources of money -- than by raising the level of cleanliness and orderliness.

Wasting, Squandering Funds

One of the best strategies for keeping a sure flow of funds is to avoid wasting money. Those who squander away funds or pay exorbitant amounts for things that can be purchased more cheaply will repel the arrival of more funds. However, if you discover what it is that you waste your money on, and overcome that habit life is likely to quickly respond with instances of good fortune.

Soft Speech

One surprising way to attract money is to control our speech. Speech is an expression of our life energy. Unfortunately, we expend a tremendous amount of nervous energy in our verbal communications; much more than is necessary to convey our thoughts. It turns out that one of the most powerful ways to attract wealth and prosperity is to reduce the volume of one's speech.

A 39-year-old wealthy American businessperson lost all 60 of his employees, and was prepared to file bankruptcy. At a relative's suggestion, he and his wife practiced the psychological and spiritual disciplines of greater attention to things, higher levels of cleanliness, bringing about greater higher harmony amongst the individuals, and soft speech. Two years later, he was in a financial position to retire for life.

When we follow the method of soft speech, or when we reduce the quantity of the words we express in our speech, we bring our own life energies under control, which create the condition for great fortune to come our way.

Changing an Attitude

A feeling or attitude is also an expression of life energy. Positive attitudes attract energy and money; negative attitudes do the opposite. If you overcome a negative attitude -- such as an unwillingness or reluctance to do something, or the harboring of bad will towards another -- new, fresh energies are released, which subtly move out into the world, returning as positive good fortune, including attraction of money.

The president of a software company was fretting about a contract he was negotiating with a client. He felt he was being pushed too hard, which raised negative feelings in him toward certain individuals at the client company. At one point, he realized that having this attitude was not helpful, so he immediately tried to block out these thoughts and feelings. Moments later, he received a check in the mail from another client for a large sum of money. It turned out to be a payment for invoice that was six months overdue; the longest overdue the company ever had.

A man changed his attitude about working weekends at a computer store. During his employment at the store, he had been at the low end of sales amongst the dozen or two salesperson working at the mini-chain. After thinking about the situation, he changed his attitude, as he saw the benefit of working on weekends. When he opened the store that Saturday, a man walked in and made a huge purchase from the salesperson, enabling him to establish the highest one-month sales of anyone in the history of the four-store franchise. As a result, he also had the highest one-month income he ever had in his life.

Dependence on Others

We always hold the power to determine our own destiny. Likewise, the real power to attract money comes from our own self-reliance, determination, and will; not from any dependence on another's help and support. The power to attract money comes from the psychological viewpoint that I am the ultimate determinant of my fate. If this is the case, then consider if you are dependent on others for funds, or similar forms of help, and change your position from one of dependence to self-dependency. Wealth and prosperity will move in your direction.

Generosity

Whenever you shift your perspective from yourself to others, energy increases, and conditions for success reveal themselves in the form of sudden and abundant positive life responses. This includes a movement on your part away from stinginess and tightfistedness, and towards generosity. Even the smallest movement in that direction can attract sudden good fortune coming your way, including the attraction of more money.

A somewhat tightfisted man decided to pay for the trip of his friend, who was in a little bit of financial stress. It was something he would not ordinarily do. The next day he received an unexpected payment for an invoice that he did not expect to arrive for quite a while.

In this event, he perceived the correlation between the overcoming of his tightness and the corresponding positive response from life. In addition, he also noted the trend that the amount he would generously give another was almost precisely equal to the amount that suddenly came back to him thereafter!

Goodwill and Generosity Too -- A related way to attract sudden good fortune is to feel goodwill and gratitude towards others. One individual inwardly sent goodwill and gratitude to various clients and friends. Soon thereafter, there was an avalanche of good news from them in terms of sales, money, and other forms of good fortune.

Focusing on, Giving Attention to the Work at Hand

We have often seen that if you focus yourself on the work at hand, i.e. what life is presenting you, rather than on the work that you would like to be doing, additional work, including fresh sources of money will fly in your direction.

An instructor taught a wide variety of software applications in his classes. One day he decided to shift his attitude from indifference to one of real concern and interest in that day's database class. Soon into the session, he noticed that the class was very upbeat and vibrant, as students were fully engaged in all manner of discussions. Then after the class, he heard from a client whom he had not heard from in years. The client was interested in having him work on a database program, which involved the very same topic area as the day's class. The new work was potentially very lucrative.

Follow the Process of Accomplishment to Rise to Higher Level in Life

A great way to attract more money is by developing a plan for improvement in your life. Decide what it is that you really want to achieve, organize the details of your vision, and carry it out with a positive attitude, and with great determination, commitment, and effort. If you follow this process, you are sure to reach your goal; i.e. success, wealth, and prosperity will come your way. Sometimes life will respond and bring you fast results even before you have made an effort. The mere decision to act can attract a response from life.

Following this process is an example of the self-conceptive power of Mind to lead our lives, rather than being led by the whims of Nature. To follow this self-directed method of improvement is to follow the fundamental process of growth and accomplishment in life. If having more money, wealth and prosperity is your goal, then following this process from beginning to end will be a full-proof method for achieving that aim.

The Ultimate Solution: Using Spirit

The single most powerful way to attract more money in your life is to use the power of Spirit. If, for example, you open yourself to the Higher Power before commencing an important activity, substantial results -- including more wealth and prosperity are likely to quickly and abundantly come your way. Often the results are simply overwhelming!

A woman, who was developing a school for children, was considering the price she was willing to pay her friend to do the work. After a discussion, she secured the somewhat lower price that she had hoped for. She then paid that amount so the work could begin. However, shortly thereafter, she reconsidered, and decided to "offer" the entire situation to the Higher Power. A very short time later, the engineer -- out of gratitude for being able to build a school for children volunteered to return all of the money he charged!

If you open to the higher spiritual power before starting an event, or when in the midst of a situation, life will respond dramatically in kind. If you also overcome a wanting attitude, life can respond overwhelmingly.

USING THE LAW OF ATTRACTION FOR MONEY EFFECTIVELY

Those who have already discovered the explosive potential within the Law of Attraction and changed their lives for the better, as well as those who are looking to uncover more about the law for the first time, usually have one thing in common – their focal point is probably money and wealth.

In today's society, being driven by a need for extraordinary wealth is often associated with greed and selfishness. The majorities of us are programmed from childhood to believe that the richest amongst us are exceptional in some way or have obtained great wealth through negative means or extreme sacrifice. However, for those who have harnessed the Law of Attraction combined with a rich person's mentality and applied it to achieve these levels of incredible wealth – income has not necessarily been their ultimate aim.

When we are looking to live out our dreams and obtain all that we want, be it good health, a business you are passionate about, a happy marriage or a life of travelling; the fact is – financial freedom must usually be obtained first. With total freedom an individual is left free to focus all of their mental energies on what it is that they truly want from life, free from the burdens and stress of bills, debts and back-breaking work. Arguably, the biggest excuse used by large numbers of unsatisfied workers is that they are unable to live out their dreams as a result of a lack of cash flow.

Very few individuals enjoy the luxury of financial freedom. However, those who have, usually have one thing in common. They are positive thinkers. They have goals and they take action. This behavior is the backbone of The Law of Attraction.

Law of Attraction and Money

It is not uncommon for those who have been enlightened by the Law Of Attraction to have accumulated great sums of wealth unknowingly. This is because being 'wealthy' should not be something which is focused on cash alone. It is possible to achieve great 'wealth' in many areas of a person's life. After all, money is simply pieces of paper and all of the paper in the world is not going to guarantee a person life-long happiness.

Those who have attracted great wealth into their life might have unlocked the powers of the Law of Attraction to attract great 'wealth' into all areas of their life – striving for inner peace and attracting positive energy into their love life, family, health and businesses. Once these things have been achieved, financial wealth is simply something can follow.

With The Law of Attraction Wealth and Abundance Can Transform Your Life

Are you blocking your own way?

Too many of us have been bought up with the understanding that great 'wealth' is something reserved for a select few people and for everyone else, financial struggle and lack is 'accepted'. Does this mindset of want and lacking sound familiar to you? If this is the case and you continually find yourself worrying about finances, bills and debt then you need to address these beliefs or lessons that were embedded in your mind within childhood. Strong and negative emotions surrounding money can come to consume your mind and how you choose to live, resulting in nothing but further money worries and a constant wanting for more.

Here is a good question to ask yourself: Have you ever known anyone that always seems at ease about money? Someone who never complains about how they cannot afford something but instead, can always buy what they wish? Someone who never gets nervous about picking up the bill or who seems to enjoy financial luck, finding $100 notes on the pavement or getting lucky with unexpected checks? These occurrences of the 'wealthy-minded' are no coincidence, they are the result of a mind that is so focused on wealth and the abundance of it, that they are openly attracting more and more of it into their life. For those who have been raised from a young age to believe that 'money doesn't grow on trees' you will notice that income does not come as easily. But why shouldn't it be readily available to you? With so much abundance in the world, how could you not enjoy the wealth that surrounds you? Re-train your perception of money and the results could be astonishing.

Find Out How to Use the Law of Attraction for Money

Did you know...? Money is energy. The world is not simply divided into those can accumulate wealth and those who will never accumulate it. Everyone has an equal chance. Those that take action and have a plan usually succeed. It is as simple as that. You are not pre-destined to a life of hardship and struggle; you alone are responsible for how much income you welcome into your life. Feel excited about money, feel thankful for what money you already have, rejoice in the knowledge that the bank of the Universe has unlimited wealth to offer you. Let your entire mind become consumed with thoughts of abundance. Make a plan that is based on something realistic and achievable and then take massive action.

THERE IS A SCIENCE FOR SUCCESS

There is a misconception in most peoples' thoughts that success, in whatever form it appears, is achieved through a God given talent, a superior intelligence or just having the fortune to be lucky in life. If only people realized that there is a science for success and it is available to anyone who seeks the knowledge to acquire it.

And that is where the problem lies, we are not taught in school how truly to become successful. We are taught in subjects that for most of our working life, we will rarely ever use and if we do, it is unlikely to benefit us to any great extent. Even our parents, unless they have an understanding of the science for success, will probably be conditioned by the same way of thinking as most of the majorities of people do also.

We are conditioned at an early age to accept certain philosophies and one of them is unless you are lucky to be left an inheritance or in these days, one of the fortunate few to win the lottery, then you must accept the common teaching of getting a good education, that leads to a stable career and save enough for a comfortable retirement. We are told being wealthy and having the riches that this will provide is just fantasy and is reserved for only the elite.

Like everything else that is going to benefit us and provide us with abundance, the truth is hidden well away from the masses. As with any science, to achieve the results we seek for our ourselves, we must first find a formula that works and follow it to gain the desired end result. The science for success is no different and many before us have implemented it into their lives and found by following a given formula, true success is well within their grasp. There is no secret to this, only the understanding and educating of ourselves.

We must get away from the type of thinking that is going to restrict us in any way and be detrimental to our future success. It is in our own hands to find the personal success we all seek. The secret is to find it, utilize it and keep on educating ourselves to the possibilities that surround each human being. The science for success is not only for the chosen few but for anyone who has the drive and desire to put it into action

INCONCLUSION

We can say that anything that we do that increases energy, attracts money; while anything that we do that depletes or squanders energy blocks money from coming our way.

Giving physical objects, systems, and people more attention, circulating money instead of squandering it, paying off current and old debts instead of ignoring them, focusing on the work at hand instead of the work you want to do, applying higher levels of cleanliness and orderliness in your home or work, changing a negative attitude towards others or towards life, using soft and reduced speech, being self-reliant and not depending on others for monetary help, moving towards generosity, goodness, and gratitude, and opening to spirit to consecrate an event are all powerful strategies for releasing energy, and attracting abundant money from life.

The power of money brings freedom. Now that I am a tad-bit "wiser" and having read many books on the subject of mindset and financial literacy I know this. You can spend your time working for money, or you can have money working for you. This concept is ignored by the ones who do not know it, and accepted and practiced by the ones who know how. Money is definitely not everything, it will not substitute family and the love that they give; but once you understand the power and positive influence that money can provide for you and for your family, it can definitely change your future for the better.

www.ingramcontent.com/pod-product-compliance
Lightning Source LLC
Chambersburg PA
CBHW050030230526
45470CB00003B/1215